Intro

Blurring the line that separates fantasy from reality, the fairy world has a mystical charm that engages us all. Each and every one of us remembers the magic of those marvellous fairytales that had such an important place in our childhood.

There are many different cultures that have created these myths, often a mixture of real beliefs and fantasy. As a result of such diverse beginnings, many different fairies have been created, such as snow fairies, fairies of the forest and mermaids, each one with its own environment and characteristics.

This book is all about the magical world full of those imaginary beings that still live in our memories. Featuring nine celebration cakes, each one with its own unique story to tell, the aim is to bring together the happiness of a special occasion with the fond childhood memories of our unforgettable fairies and their tales that began, *"Once upon a time…"*

Cecilia Morana

Dedication

To Camila, my little granddaughter.

Acknowledgements

I wish to thank my husband for all his support.

I wish also to thank my Swedish friend, Agneta Olsson, for her trust and help and to express my gratitude to Beverley and Robert Dutton for their trust.

Finally, I would like to thank my assistants Patricia Cabaza, Catalina Calcagno, María Maldonado, Laura González, Silvia Prychodzko, Mónica López, Laura Álvarez and Lidia Sinni.

Contents

Cakes:

Edibles and Equipment

A list of the materials and equipment required is given for each project. However, there are several items which are used throughout the book, so it is worth having these to hand before you start.

Edibles

• Sugarpaste (rolled fondant), a ready-to-roll icing that is used to cover cakes.

• Flower paste/SFP (gum paste), an edible paste that is used for making flowers, fabric effects and small figures.

• Royal icing, which is piped onto sugar work to create various effects using different nozzles (e.g. hair for fairies) and is also used to secure sugar pieces together.

• Pastillage, a paste which dries hard, making it ideal for creating sugar structures where strength is required. It can also be used to make rock sugar (see pages 4 to 5).

• Mexican Modelling Paste (MMP), a soft, malleable paste that is used for figure modelling.

• Dust food colours, which are brushed onto the surface of sugar work to give a subtle effect, e.g. to blush the cheeks of a fairy. They can also be mixed with clear alcohol to make a quick-drying paint.

• Liquid food colours, which can be painted directly onto sugar work and can be used in an airbrush to create a soft, graduated effect. If you do not have an airbrush, you can use dust colours to create similar effects.

• Paste food colours, which are ideal for colouring royal icing and pastes such as sugarpaste, modelling paste, flower paste and pastillage (colours must be glycerine-free).

Equipment

- Selection of metal or plastic modelling tools
- Good quality metal cutters (see Fantasy Flowers and Leaves on pages 9 to 11)
- SK Great Impressions Petal and Leaf Veiners (see Fantasy Flowers and Leaves on pages 9 to 11)
- SK Great Impressions Face Moulds (see How to Make a Fairy on pages 6 to 9)
- Floristry tape in various colours
- Wires and wire cutters
- Good quality, durable paintbrushes, ranging in size
- Non-stick polythene board and rolling pins: large and small
- Sharp knife/scalpel and fine, pointed scissors

> **IMPORTANT NOTE**
> All of the cakes in this book include items which are either inedible (e.g. nylon thread, wires and cocktail stick) or are edible but should not be eaten (e.g. raw, dried spaghetti). All such items are a choking hazard and must be removed before the cake is served. If the cake is a gift, always ensure the recipient is aware that these items must be removed before the cake is served.

Basic Techniques

Covering a Cake Board (Drum)

1. Dust a non-stick board with icing sugar to prevent the sugarpaste from sticking.

2. Using a large rolling pin, roll out the sugarpaste to a thickness of approximately 3mm ($^1/_8$"). Ensure the paste is slightly larger than the board to be covered.

3. Using a pastry brush, lightly moisten the board with cooled, boiled water. Carefully fold the paste over the rolling pin to prevent stretching and lift the paste onto the board.

4. Gently smooth over the paste with a cake smoother. Trim away the excess paste from around the edge of the board using a sharp knife.

5. To finish, secure a length of ribbon around the edge of the board using a non-toxic glue stick or double-sided tape. Ensure the ribbon join is at the back when positioning the cake on the board.

Covering a Cake

Throughout the book, I have used Madeira cakes and covered them with sugarpaste using the following method:

1. Spread a thin layer of buttercream or jam over the surface of the cake. This will help the sugarpaste to stick.

2. Roll out the sugarpaste on a non-stick board dusted with icing sugar (as above). Ensure the paste is large enough to cover the top and sides of the cake.

3. Carefully fold the paste over the rolling pin to prevent stretching and lift the paste onto the cake. Gently smooth the paste down the sides of the cake using the palm of your hand, taking care not to stretch and crack the paste. Gently smooth the paste over any corners and curves, then use a cake smoother to achieve a professional finish.

4. Using a sharp knife, trim the excess paste away from the base of the cake and smooth again using the smoother.

5. Lift the cake by sliding a large palette knife underneath it and place it onto the covered board. You can eliminate any finger marks using the cake smoother.

Making Rock Sugar

This technique is used to make irregular shapes for the rocks and corals in The Mermaid Ball (see pages 45 to 47). Traditionally, rock sugar is made by boiling sugar (see Method 1) but it can also be made in the microwave to save time (Method 2).

Method 1: Sugar Boiling

Ingredients

450g (1lb) granulated sugar
200ml (7fl oz) cooled, boiled water
30g (1oz) royal icing

Equipment

Large saucepan with lid
Wooden spatula
Metal tray

1. Make sure all the equipment is clean and free from grease. Pour the sugar into a large saucepan and saturate with water. Make sure that the pan is no more than one third full.

2. Heat the sugar solution to boiling temperature, i.e. 138°C. Wash down the sides of the saucepan occasionally with a wooden spatula or pastry brush to help the sugar boil evenly. Colour may be added at this stage if required.

3. When the mixture reaches 138°C, immediately remove the saucepan from the heat and stir in the royal icing. Place a tight-fitting lid on the saucepan as soon as the icing has blended into the sugar and return to a low heat.

4. After a few minutes the sugar will rise to the top of the saucepan. As soon as this occurs, remove the saucepan from the heat (do not leave the solution on the heat for too long as this will discolour the sugar). As soon as you have removed the pan from the heat, turn the sugar out onto a metal tray. Break up the sugar into pieces, as required.

5. Place the sugar rocks in a cake box or similar and store in a cool, dry place.

Method 2: Microwave

Ingredients
Small amount of pastillage

Equipment
Dish for microwave

1. Place a small ball of pastillage into a dish suitable for use in a microwave. Heat on full power for approximately 4 or 5 minutes, checking regularly. The cooking time will depend on the power of the microwave and the amount of pastillage.

2. Remove the pastillage from the microwave and break into pieces.

3. Place the sugar rocks in a cake box or similar and store in a cool, dry place.

How to Make a Fairy

The fairies that are featured in this book are all made following the same basic method. Each fairy is then adapted to create the individual characters that are represented in the projects.

Materials

Flesh-coloured flower paste (see below)

SK QFC Pastes: various

SK QFC Dusts: various

SK Glaze Cleaner (IPA) or clear alcohol (e.g. gin or vodka)

Dried spaghetti strands

Equipment

SK Great Impressions Face Moulds: Extra Small, Small, Medium and Large

Set of 2 fairy wings (see page 8)

SK Paintbrushes: nos. 00 and 0

SK Dusting Brush

CelStick

Colouring the Paste

To make the skin tone for the fairies, colour a piece of White SFP with a hint of Orange and Pink QFC Pastes. You will need the following quantities of paste for each size of fairy:

Large: 90g

Medium: 45g

Small: 20g

Extra Small: 10g

Note: These quantities are enough to make an entire fairy, so if you are making the body or limbs in a different colour, take this off the total amount. It is always advisable to colour too much paste rather than too little as it can be difficult to match the original colour when making a second batch.

Body

1. Take the required amount of flower paste for the size of fairy you are making (see above) and use approximately one third of this to make the body.

2. Roll the paste into a cone, then squeeze in the middle to create a waist.

3. Gently flatten the body and soften any curves.

Head

There are two methods for making the head: you can either use the range of SK Great Impressions Face Moulds or model it by hand.

Method 1: using a mould

1. Roll a ball of flesh-coloured flower paste, ensuring there is enough paste to fill the mould (approximately one sixth of the total amount required for the fairy).

2. Push the paste into the mould, applying pressure to ensure that the features are well defined. Round off the back of the head.

3. Carefully remove the paste from the mould, pulling it from the neck area to avoid distorting the face. Insert a length of dried spaghetti into the neck – this will support the head when it is attached to the body. Allow to dry.

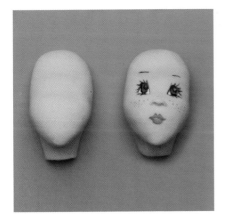

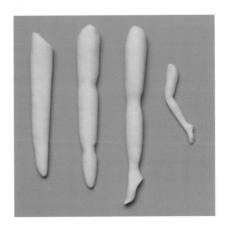

Method 2: modelling by hand

1. Roll a small ball of flesh-coloured flower paste: you will need approximately one sixth of the total amount required for each fairy size (see above).

2. Push into the centre with your little finger. This will create a hollow area where the eyes will be.

3. Squeeze the paste at the base of the head and pull down to create the neck.

4. Model a small nose and attach it just below the hollow area.

5. Insert a length of dried spaghetti into the neck – this will support the head when it is attached to the body. Allow to dry.

Painting the Face

To create the detail on the fairy's face, you will need to dilute a selection of SK QFC Dusts with either SK Glaze Cleaner (IPA) or clear spirit such as gin or vodka to create fast-drying, edible paint. Avoid using too much liquid and always dab any excess paint onto kitchen towel before applying to the face.

1. Paint the whites of the eyes and allow to dry. Paint the irises over the top in your chosen colour.

2. Using a very fine brush (no. 00), paint the eyelashes in brown or black and paint the pupils in black.

3. Paint the lips in pink (using a mixture of SK Pink and Red QFC Dusts), starting from the centre and working out to the edge to ensure the mouth is central.

4. Blush the cheeks with a little pink QFC Dust using a dry dusting brush.

Legs

1. Using approximately one third of the paste required for the entire fairy (see opposite), roll a sausage of flesh-coloured flower paste and taper at one end.

2. Position your little finger at the ankle and roll the paste half a turn whilst pressing gently to narrow the paste slightly.

3. Position your little finger at the knee and roll in the same way to narrow the paste. Ensure that the contours of the leg are smooth.

4. Gently bend the foot and leg into the required position.

5. Using a CelStick, mark the toes. Use your fingers to create the bridge of the foot.

6. Repeat to make a second leg.

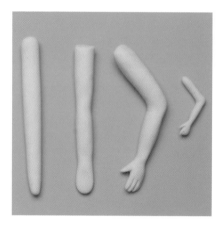

Arms

The method for making the arms is similar to the method for making the legs but you will require a shorter cylinder of paste (approximately one fifth of the total amount; the arms should reach mid-thigh level with the elbow at waist height.)

1. Roll a sausage of paste to the required length. Using your little finger, narrow the paste at the wrist in the same way as before, this time rotating the paste one complete turn. Make the elbow with a half-turn.

2. Shape the hands by flattening the paste slightly. Using fine scissors, snip off a small triangle of paste, separating the thumb from the fingers.

3. Make three more cuts to create the four fingers. Make sure these cuts go down to just above the thumb. Gently shape the hand into the required position.

4. Make the second arm and hand in the same way and bend both arms into position.

5. Allow to firm, then attach the arms with edible glue.

Wings

The wings of the fairies are made using gelatine, following the instructions below. Petals and leaves can also be made using the same method.

Ingredients

10ml (2tsp) cooled, boiled water

5g (1 level tsp) powdered gelatine

Pinch of SK Metallic Lustre Dust: Snowflake

SK QFC Paste in a colour of your choice

Equipment

Thin, white floristry wire

Polystyrene block

Method

1. Put the water and gelatine into a bowl and stir until the water has absorbed the gelatine.

2. Add the SK Snowflake Metallic Lustre Dust and the desired SK Paste Food Colour to the gelatine mixture. Make sure you add the colours slowly, to avoid the formation of air bubbles.

3. Heat the mixture gently in a bain-marie until the gelatine has fully dissolved.

4. Using a thin, white floristry wire, make the shape required for the wing (or petal). Twist the ends together firmly, leaving a length of wire to hold.

5. Slowly submerge the wire shape in the gelatine mixture and then slowly remove it. Check that the shape has a thin gelatine film: if the film collapses or does not form, simply dip the wire back into the mixture again.

6. Push the end of the wire into a block of polystyrene and allow the gelatine to set for at least 1 hour.

Fantasy Flowers and Leaves

Several different stylised flowers and leaves have been used alongside the fairies in this book.
The flowers can be any colour to complement the colours on the cake –
here, I have shown one colour here as an example of each flower.
I have shown and numbered the cutters used to create these flowers and included a veiner where
necessary, but it is not essential that they match exactly – you can use similar cutters and veiners that
you may already have in your sugarcraft kit.

Materials

Flower paste
SK QFC Dusts: various
Cornflour

Equipment

Non-stick board and small rolling pin
Ball tool
CelStick
Flower and leaf cutters (as specified below)
SK Great Impressions Veiners (as specified below)
Nylon thread
PVA glue

Fantasy Flower 1

Cutter: Tinkertech Two Calyx no. 406

1. Make a small Mexican hat shape from flower paste and stand it upright on a non-stick board. Roll out the base to thin out the paste.

2. Cut out a flower shape using cutter no. 1. Mark the centre with a CelStick and open up the throat of the flower. Make one mark in each petal.

3. Make your own pollen by mixing a little QFC Paste (I have used Yellow and Pink) with some cornflour. Take a piece of nylon thread, dip one end in PVA glue and then into the pollen colour.

4. Pull the single stamen down through the centre of the flower and cut to the required length.

Fantasy Flower 2

Cutter: Tinkertech Two Petunia no. 599

Veiner: SK Great Impressions Sweet Pea

1. Make a small Mexican hat shape from flower paste. Roll out the base to thin out the paste.

2. Cut out a flower shape using cutter no. 2. Mark the centre with a CelStick and open up the throat. Mark each petal with a veiner.

3. Cut a length of nylon thread to make 5 stamens. Dip one end of each stamen in PVA glue and then in your chosen QFC Dust (I have used Pink).

4. Cut a piece of 24-gauge green floristry wire and tape the stamens around the wire with green floristry tape. Push the stamens through the centre of the flower and pull down.

5. Dust the petals with shades of Pink Dust Colour.

Fantasy Flower 3

Cutter: Tinkertech Two Hyacinth, no. 303

1. Make a small Mexican hat shape from flower paste. Roll out the base to thin out the paste.

2. Cut out a flower shape using cutter no. 3. Mark the centre with a CelStick and open up the throat. Run a ball tool along the back of each petal to thin the paste and curl the petals back.

3. Make 1 stamen from a piece of nylon thread. Dip one end in PVA glue and then in your chosen colour (I have used Blue QFC Dust).

4. Cut a piece of 24-gauge green floristry wire and tape the stamen around the wire with green floristry tape.

5. Dust the petals with shades of Blue QFC Dust.

Fantasy Flower 4

Cutter: Tinkertech Two Banks Rose, no. 664

1. Make a small Mexican hat shape from flower paste. Roll out the base to thin out the paste.

2. Cut out a flower shape with cutter no. 4. Mark the centre with a CelStick.

3. Cut 5 lengths of nylon thread for the stamens, dip one end into PVA glue and then in your chosen colour (I have used White QFC Dust).

4. Cut a piece of 26-gauge green floristry wire and tape the stamens around the wire with green floristry tape.

Fantasy Flower 5

Cutter: Tinkertech Two Fantasy Flower no. 968

1. Roll out a piece of flower paste and cut out the flower shape with cutter no. 5. Cup the back of each petal with a ball tool.

2. Cut 5 lengths of nylon thread for the stamens, dip one end into PVA glue and then into your chosen dust colour (I have used white, yellow and orange). Cut a piece of 24-gauge green floristry wire and tape the stamens around the wire with green floristry tape.

3. Dust the petals with touches of white, yellow and orange. If desired, add small dots of SK Bordeaux Dust Food Colour mixed with glaze cleaner (IPA) or clear alcohol.

Fantasy Leaf 1

Cutters: Tinkertech Two Daisy Leaf nos. 445 (medium) and 530 (small)

The large leaf requires a template (see inside back cover)

Veiner: SK Great Impressions Honeysuckle

Fantasy Leaf 2

Cutters: Tinkertech Two Fantasy Leaf, nos. 965 (extra large), 966 (large), 967 (medium), and Ivy no. 581 (small)

Veiner: SK Great Impressions Anemone Leaf

1. Roll out some flower paste and cut out the leaf shape with your chosen cutter or template. Texture the leaf using the corresponding veiner, leaving a ridge down the centre.

2. To wire each leaf, dip the end of a floristry wire into edible glue and insert the glued end into the central vein. Use a 26-gauge wire for each small leaf, a 24-gauge wire for each medium leaf and a 22-gauge wire for each large leaf. Push the wire approximately halfway up the leaf. (You will not need to wire all the leaves as some are just placed in position.)

3. Gently bend the leaf to the required shape and allow to dry.

Dancing in the Woods

Materials

25.5cm (10") hexagonal cake
250g (9oz) SK Sugar Florist Paste (SFP): White
1kg (2lb 3oz) green sugarpaste
450g (1lb) SK Marzipan
SK QFC Dusts: Black, Brown, Green, Orange, Pink,
Red, White and Yellow
SK QFC Pastes: Black, Brown, Green, Orange, Pink,
Red, White and Yellow
SK Professional Liquid or Dust Colour: Bulrush
SK Fairy Dust: Ice White
SK Edible Glue
Gelatine solution (see pages 8 to 9)
Royal icing
Raw, dried spaghetti

Equipment

Non-stick board and rolling pin
Airbrush (optional)
SK Great Impressions Face Mould: Small
New, clean nailbrush
SK Paintbrushes: nos. 00 and 4
Fine scissors
CelStick
Fantasy flower cutters: nos. 1, 2 and 4 (see pages
9 to 11)
Fantasy leaf cutter: no. 1, medium
SK Great Impressions Sweet Pea Veiner
Butterfly cutter/template (see inside back cover)
24-gauge floristry wires: green
Wire cutters
Floristry tape: green
2 bowls
Piping nozzles: nos. 2 and 3
Piping bag
Stamens: white
PVA glue
30.5cm (12") hexagonal cake drum
50cm x 1.5mm width ribbon: dark green

Method

Covering the Cake and Board

1. Cover the cake and board with green sugarpaste. Place the cake in the centre of the board. Trim the board with dark green ribbon.

2. Texture the centre of the cake with a new, clean nailbrush or a food-grade texture mat before the sugarpaste has dried.

Dancing Fairies

For instructions on how to make a fairy, see pages 6 to 9.

1. Make four small fairy bodies in green SFP.

2. Make the head, arms and legs for each of the fairies in flesh-coloured SFP. Bend the arms and legs slightly so that the fairies look like they are dancing.

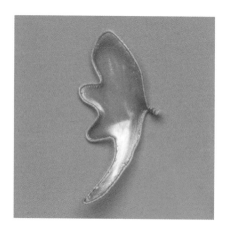

3. Paint the faces with diluted QFC Dusts using a fine paintbrush.

4. Allow all the pieces to dry, then secure them together with royal icing.

5. To make the dresses, you will need 16 petals for each fairy. Thinly roll out some White SFP and cut out 32 individual petals using the no. 4 fantasy flower cutter. Repeat the same process with pale pink SFP and secure the petals around the fairies' waists with royal icing, making two pink skirts and two white skirts.

6. Roll out a long strip of green SFP and cut a fringe with a pair of fine scissors. Secure around the neck and waist of each fairy.

7. Make the wings using the gelatine technique, following the template (see inside back cover). Add Pink QFC Paste to the solution to give the wings colour. When dry, secure to the back of the fairies.

8. Make some royal icing and divide into two bowls. Colour one brown and the other yellow.

Place the yellow icing into a piping bag with a no. 3 nozzle and pipe the hair of one of the fairies. Repeat the same method for two other fairies using the brown coloured icing, then add a little black to this and pipe the hair of the fourth fairy. Use a dampened no. 4 paintbrush to smooth the hair and give it movement.

Mushrooms

1. Divide the marzipan to make the mushrooms: you will need approximately

two thirds of the marzipan for the large mushroom and the remaining third for the smaller one.

2. Make a cylinder for the stalk of the large mushroom. Texture the surface of the paste with a CelStick.

3. Insert a length of raw spaghetti down through the stem, leaving some protruding from the top. This will give added support.

4. To make the cap, roll a ball of marzipan, then flatten the base and pull down the sides with your fingers. Mark lines down the sides with a CelStick. Position the cap on the stem, using the spaghetti as support. Use a little edible glue to join the two pieces together.

5. Make the second, smaller mushroom in the same way. Airbrush both mushrooms with Bulrush Liquid Colour, or dust with Bulrush Dust if you do not have an airbrush.

Flowers, Stones and Grass

1. I have used fantasy flowers 1, 2 and 4 on this cake, plus a medium no. 1 fantasy

leaf (see pages 9 to 11). You will need approximately 24 of flower no. 1 in yellow with red stamens, eight of flower no. 2 in pink with orange and yellow stamens, and seven of flower no. 4 in white with green stamens. You will need to make approximately 12 pale green, medium no. 1 leaves.

2. Wire the flowers and leaves together in small groups for the top and base of the cake. Some flowers can be displayed singly and left unwired.

3. To make the stones, colour some SFP unevenly with Black and Brown QFC Paste Colours. Roll small, uneven balls and allow to firm.

4. Paint the grass onto the sides of the cake using Green QFC Paste a no. 4 paintbrush. Allow to dry.

Butterflies

1. Roll out some White SFP thinly. Cut out two sets of butterfly wings and allow to dry on a former to give the wings movement.

2. Using diluted QFC Dusts, paint the butterflies in shades of red, brown, yellow and green.

3. Roll a sausage of SFP for each body and secure the wings to the body with royal icing. Support the wings until dry.

4. Make two anthers for each butterfly from white stamens. Dip the ends into PVA glue, then in Orange QFC Dust and attach to the body.

Assembly

1. Position the mushrooms in the centre of the cake and secure with royal icing.

2. Arrange clusters of flowers on each corner of the cake and around the base. Secure stones around the base of the cake to hide the join. Add a few flowers around the board.

3. Place the dancing fairies in position. Secure several stones around the foot of each fairy to hold it in place.

4. Place one butterfly on a flower and the other on the large mushroom.

Fairy Blossoms

Materials

3 x 12.5cm (5") round cakes

250g (9oz) SK Sugar Florist Paste (SFP): White

1kg (2lb 3oz) sugarpaste: white

SK QFC Dusts: Blue, Pink, Purple and White

SK QFC Pastes: Black, Blue, Brown, Green, Orange, Pink, Purple, Red, White and Yellow

SK Fairy Dust: Ice White

SK Glaze Cleaner (IPA)

Gelatine solution (see pages 8 to 9)

Royal icing

Equipment

Non-stick board and rolling pin

SK Great Impressions Face Mould: Medium

SK Paintbrushes: nos. 00, 4 and 10 (for dusting)

Rose petal cutters: large and small

Piping nozzle: no. 3

Piping bag

Fine scissors

Ball tool

3 x 15cm (6") round cake drums

50cm (20") x 1.5cm width ribbons: blue, pink and purple

Method

Covering the Cakes and Boards

Divide the sugarpaste into three equal pieces and colour with Blue, Pink and Purple QFC Pastes. Cover the cakes and boards and place each cake centrally on the corresponding board. Trim the cakes and boards with the corresponding ribbon and allow to firm.

Fairies

For instructions on how to make a fairy, see pages 6 to 9.

1. Make three medium bodies from green-coloured SFP.

2. Make the heads, arms and legs in flesh-coloured SFP for the three fairies. Bend the arms and legs into natural poses.

3. Paint the faces with diluted QFC Dusts using a no. 00 paintbrush.

4. Allow all the pieces to dry. When dry, assemble the fairies using royal icing.

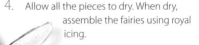

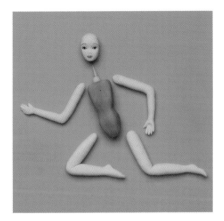

5. Colour 150g of SFP the same colour as each cake to make the skirt and rose petals. Roll out the paste thinly and cut out 16 petals for each skirt using a small rose petal cutter or template. Secure the petals around the waist of each fairy, creating two layers. Gently lift the edges of the top layer to give movement.

6. Make the wings using the gelatine technique, following the template as a guide (see inside back cover). When you are preparing the gelatine, add some Pink QFC Paste to the solution.

7. Roll out a strip of green-coloured SFP and cut into the paste with fine scissors to form a fringe. Secure the fringe around the neck and waist of each fairy.

8. Make some royal icing, divide it into three bowls and colour it yellow, brown and black. Put each colour in a piping bag with a no. 3 nozzle and pipe the hair of each fairy. Use a no. 4 paintbrush dampened with cooled, boiled water to smooth the hair.

Roses

1. Use the SFP coloured earlier to make the skirts. Roll out the paste thinly and cut out 11 large petals and 11 smaller petals for each rose using the cutters.

2. Soften the edges of the petals with a ball tool.

3. Using a dusting brush, dust the petals with the corresponding colour. Colour the smaller petals a strong tone and the larger petals a lighter tone. Add some dust colour around the top edge of the cake to soften the overall effect.

4. Secure the large petals to the cakes, working round in a circle and overlapping them slightly. Add the smaller petals on top.

5. Finally, secure a fairy to the cakes in the centre of each rose using royal icing.

Snow Fairy

Materials

25.5cm (10") round cake

500g (1lb 1oz) pastillage

250g (9oz) Sugar Florist Paste (SFP): White

1kg (2lb 3oz) sugarpaste: white

SK QFC Dusts: Blue, Brown, Pink, Red and White

SK Metallic Lustre Dust: Snowflake

SK QFC Pastes: Pink, Orange

SK Professional Liquid or Dust Food Colour: Gentian

SK Fairy Dust: Ice White

SK Glaze Cleaner (IPA)

Gelatine solution (see pages 8 to 9)

Royal icing

Equipment

Non-stick board and rolling pin

Airbrush (optional)

SK Great Impressions Face Mould: Large

Scissors

Sharp knife

Modelling tools (PME)

SK Paintbrushes: nos. 00 and 6

Snowflake mould (CelCakes)

55cm (20") 24-gauge floristry wires

Wire cutters

Piping nozzles: nos. 4 and 40

Piping bag

30.5cm (12") round cake drum

50cm x 1.5cm (20" x ½") width ribbon: white

20.5cm diameter x 8cm depth (8" x 3") round polystyrene dummy

Method

Covering the Cake

1. Cover the cake and board with white sugarpaste and allow to firm. Trim the board with white ribbon.

2. Cover the dummy with white sugarpaste in the same way, position centrally on the board and place the cake on top. This will lift the cake away from the base board.

Snow Fairy

For instructions on how to make a fairy, see pages 6 to 9.

1. Make the body of the fairy from 30g of White SFP.

2. Colour 60g of flower paste a flesh tone using a hint of Pink and Orange QFC Pastes. Make the face, arms and legs. Bend the legs so that the fairy is in a kneeling position.

3. Using a fine paintbrush, paint the face with QFC Dusts mixed with glaze cleaner.

4. Allow all the pieces to dry. When dry, secure the pieces together with royal icing.

5. To make the dress, thinly roll out a piece of white flower paste to resemble fabric. Cut out several diamonds and pointed shapes, following the step photograph as a guide. Stick the pieces around the neck and waist to create the blouse and skirt.

6. Make the wings using the gelatine technique, following the top and bottom parts of the template (see inside back cover). Add some Snowflake Metallic Lustre Dust to the gelatine mixture; no colour is required.

7. Place some royal icing in a piping bag with a no. 4 piping nozzle. Pipe the hair onto the head. Dampen a no. 6 paintbrush with cooled, boiled water and use it to smooth the hair and give it movement.

8. Sprinkle Fairy Dust over the dress.

Ice Shards and Snowflakes

1. Roll out the pastillage to a thickness of approximately 2mm. Cut out the shards of ice in different sizes using the templates (see inside back cover).

2. Allow the pastillage pieces to dry on a curved former. Once the pieces are completely dry, lightly airbrush them with Gentian Liquid Colour, gradually fading the colour towards the top. If you do

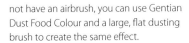

not have an airbrush, you can use Gentian Dust Food Colour and a large, flat dusting brush to create the same effect.

3. Use the mould to make several snowflakes. Allow to dry, then dust the snowflakes with Fairy Dust.

Assembly

1. Stick the shards of ice to the board with royal icing.

2. Place the fairy in the centre of the cake. Secure more shards of ice in an arc to surround and protect her.

3. Stick snowflakes in random positions on the cake.

4. Place some royal icing into a piping bag with a no. 40 nozzle. Pipe little snowballs all over the cake, adding more at the base of the ice shards to give extra support.

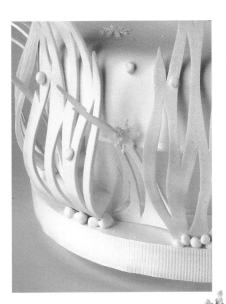

River Fairy

Materials

30.5cm (12") round cake
250g (9oz) Sugar Florist Paste (SFP): White
1.5kg (3lb 3oz) sugarpaste: white
SK QFC Dusts: Black, Blue, Brown, Red and White
SK QFC Liquids: Orange and Red
SK QFC Pastes: Black, Blue, Brown, Green, Orange, Pink and Yellow
SK Professional Liquid or Dust Food Colour: Gentian
SK Fairy Dust: Ice White
SK Edible Gold Paint
Royal icing
SK Glaze Cleaner (IPA)
SK Confectioners' Glaze
SK Piping Gel
Gelatine solution (see pages 8 to 9)

Equipment

Non-stick board and rolling pin
Airbrush (optional)
SK Great Impressions Face Mould: Large
Sharp knife
Modelling tools (PME)
SK Paintbrushes: nos. 00, 4 and 6
Tiny blossom cutter (OP, no. F2S)
Fantasy flower cutters: nos. 3 and 4 (see pages 9 to 11)
26-gauge floristry wire: green
Floristry tape: green
Wire cutters
Piping nozzle: no. 4
Piping bag
Nylon thread
PVA glue
Irregularly shaped mirror (for base)

Method

Covering the Cake

1. Carve the round cake into an oval shape, measuring approximately 25.5cm x 30.5cm (10" x 12"). Keep the remaining pieces of cake as these will be used to create the waterfall. Reserve a small piece of white sugarpaste and colour the rest a pale green shade. Cover the oval cake with the pale green sugarpaste and place centrally on the mirror base.

2. Assemble the small pieces of cake to create the waterfall shape. Cover the front with the pale green sugarpaste and the back with brown-coloured sugarpaste. Place the waterfall on the cake.

3. Using an airbrush with Gentian Liquid Colour or Gentian Dust Colour and a flat brush, add blue tinges over the cake and waterfall.

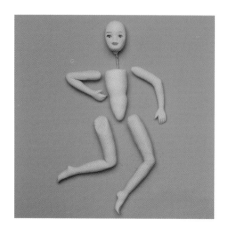

Rocks and Water

1. Colour some SFP a brown/grey colour and model several rocks and stones. Position some of the smaller stones around the waterfall, place some around the base of the cake, and make a pile of rocks for the fairy to sit on.

2. Pour the piping gel down the waterfall, over the top of the cake, down the sides and around the mirrored board. Using a brush, apply the gel to the grass and stones as if the water is running over them.

River Fairy

For instructions on how to make a fairy, see pages 6 to 9.

1. Make a large body in SFP (you can use any colour as it will be covered).

2. Make the face, arms and legs from flesh coloured SFP. Bend the legs into a sitting position and bend the right arm.

3. Paint the face with diluted QFC Dust Colours using a fine paintbrush. Give the fairy a pale complexion and blue eyes.

4. Allow all the pieces dry. When dry, secure

the pieces together with royal icing. (Do not attach the arms at this stage.)

5. Colour some SFP with a hint of Blue QFC Paste to make a sky blue colour. Roll the paste out thinly and cut out a rectangle. Pleat the paste along the top edge to make the dress and carefully position it on the fairy's body, draping the fabric over her legs.

6. Make two sleeves in the same way and attach to the arms. Secure the arms to the body using royal icing.

7. Make the wings using the gelatine

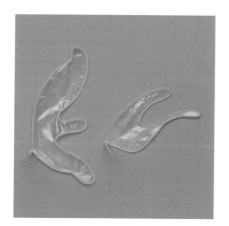

technique, following the template (see inside back cover). No colour should be used for the wings.

8. Colour a small amount of royal icing with Yellow QFC Paste and pipe the hair using a no. 4 nozzle. Dampen a no. 6 paintbrush with cooled, boiled water and use it to smooth the hair and give it movement. Allow the icing to dry, then paint the ends of the hair with diluted Red and Orange QFC Liquids. Cut out several small blossoms and secure to the head whilst the icing is still wet.

9. Sprinkle Fairy Dust over the dress.

10. Model a tiny hairbrush from SFP and gild with Edible Gold Paint. Allow to dry, then secure it in the hand of the fairy with royal icing.

Flowers and Pebbles

1. To make the blue flowers, colour some SFP with Blue QFC Paste. Make fantasy flower no. 3, following the instructions on pages 9 to 11. Add a single blue stamen, then tape each flower to a no. 26 wire. Make 15 altogether.

2. To make the white flowers, roll out some White SFP and follow the instructions for making flower no. 4 (see pages 9 to 11). Cut seven 3cm pieces of nylon thread and make blue stamens for each flower. Make ten altogether and then tape each flower to a no. 26 wire.

3. Make approximately eight medium no. 1 fantasy leaves in green SFP (see pages 9 to 11).

4. Secure the flowers and leaves around the cake, waterfall and base in small groups.

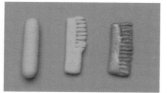

Fairy of the Forest

Materials

25.5cm (10") round cake

350g (12oz) SK Sugar Florist Paste (SFP): White

1kg (2lb 3oz) sugarpaste: green

SK QFC Pastes: Blue, Brown, Green, Orange and Pink

SK QFC Dusts: Black, Blue, Pink and White

SK Professional Liquid or Dust Food Colours: Bulrush, Daffodil, Mint and Poinsettia

SK Fairy Dust: Ice White

Royal icing

SK Confectioners' Glaze

Gelatine solution (see pages 8 to 9)

Equipment

Non-stick board and rolling pin

Airbrush (optional)

SK Great Impressions Face Mould: Large

Sharp knife

SK Paintbrushes: nos. 00 and 4

Fantasy leaf cutters and template: nos. 1 and 2, large, medium and small (see pages 9 to 11)

SK Great Impressions Leaf Moulds: Anemone and Honeysuckle

24-gauge floristry wire: green

Floristry tape: brown and green

Wire cutters

Piping nozzle: no. 4

Piping bag

30.5cm (12") round cake drum

50cm (20") x 1.5mm width ribbon: dark green

Method

Covering the Cake and Board

1. Cover the board with green sugarpaste.

2. Carve a semicircle out of the round cake to make a crescent shape. Cover the cake with green sugarpaste and allow to firm. Place the cake centrally on the board and trim the board with dark green ribbon.

Fairy of the Forest

For instructions on how to make a fairy, see pages 6 to 9.

1. Make a large fairy body in green SFP.

2. Make the face, arms and legs in flesh-coloured SFP. Bend the legs so that the fairy is in a kneeling position.

3. Paint the face with diluted QFC Dusts using a fine paintbrush. This fairy has blue eyes and pale lips.

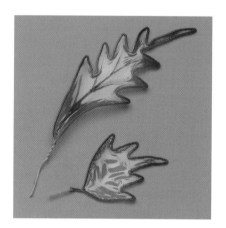

4. Allow the pieces to dry, and then secure them together with royal icing.

5. Colour some SFP with Green QFC Paste and roll out thinly. Using a medium no. 1 fantasy leaf cutter (see pages 9 to 11), cut out approximately 15 leaves and secure them around the fairy's waist to make a skirt. Using a small no. 1 fantasy leaf cutter, cut out five leaves and secure them around the neck. Cut out a further five small leaves and set aside to dry.

6. Make the wings using the gelatine technique, following the template (see inside back cover). Colour the gelatine by adding a little Green QFC Paste. Allow to dry.

7. Colour some royal icing a chestnut brown colour using a mixture of Brown and Orange QFC Pastes. Put the icing in a piping bag with a no. 4 nozzle and pipe the hair. Use a no. 4 paintbrush dampened with cooled, boiled water to smooth the hair and give it movement. Position the five small leaves made earlier on top of the head whilst the icing is still soft.

Leaves and Branches

1. Using several different leaf cutters, make a selection of leaves from green-coloured SFP. Add varying degrees of colour to give a variety of green tones.

2. Insert a green wire into the back of some of the leaves and leave some unwired. Place the leaves on a former with some curled up and allow to dry.

3. Tape some of the leaves together to form small stems, with the smallest leaves at the top.

4. To make the small branches, cut small pieces of brown floristry tape and twist them. Group several pieces of twisted tape together and twist them around a length of floristry wire to add strength. Arrange the branches as desired using your fingers.

Airbrushing and Assembly

1. Position the leaves and branches against the covered cake and airbrush or dust them in different tones of brown, green, red and yellow. Change the position of the leaves and airbrush or dust again. Repeat this process to create an irregular pattern, representing the forest floor. Allow to dry.

2. Place the fairy in the centre of the cake. Arrange the leaves and branches around the fairy, securing them to the cake with royal icing. Where there are wires, do not push them into the cake: bend the end into a right angle, secure this to the cake with royal icing and cover with a leaf.

3. Cover the join between the cake and the board with leaves and branches. Make stones from leftover pieces of paste and secure these to the board and around the base of the cake.

Make a Wish

Materials

30.5 x 25.5cm (12" x 10") oval cake
250g (9oz) SK Sugar Florist Paste: White
250g (9oz) pastillage
1kg (2lb 3oz) sugarpaste: pale pink
SK QFC Dusts: Black, Blue, Brown, Pink, Red, White and Yellow
SK QFC Pastes: Black, Blue, Brown, Orange, Pink, Purple, Red, White and Yellow
SK Glaze Cleaner (IPA)
SK Fairy Dust: Ice White
Gelatine solution (see pages 8 to 9)
Royal icing
Raw, dried spaghetti

Equipment

Non-stick board and rolling pin
Fantasy flower cutters: nos. 1, 2, 3 and 4 (see pages 9 to 11)
SK Great Impressions Sweet Pea Veiner
Fantasy leaf cutters: no. 1 medium and small
SK Great Impressions Honeysuckle Veiner
Heart cutter (TT, no. 328 from set 327-330)
Tiny blossom cutter (OP, no. F2S)
24-and 26-gauge floristry wires: green
Floristry tape: green
Wire cutters
SK Paintbrushes: nos. 00 and 4
Piping nozzle: no. 5
Piping bag
Knife or ruler
Stamens: white
35.5cm x 30.5cm (14" x 12") oval cake drum
55cm (21") x 1.5cm width ribbon: pink (to trim board)
45cm (18") wide decorative ribbon: pink (to trim cake)

Method

Covering the Cake and Board

1. Cover the cake and board with pale pink sugarpaste. Allow to firm, then place the cake centrally on the board. Trim the board with pink ribbon.

2. Cover the join between the cake and board by securing a length of decorative pink ribbon around the base of the cake. Tie in a bow at the front.

Window

1. Roll out the pastillage to a thickness of 3mm and cut out the back part of the window using the template (see inside back cover). Dust lightly with Pink QFC Dust.

2. Colour the remaining pastillage with a hint of Brown QFC Paste and roll out to a thickness of 3mm. Using the template, cut out the two parts of the window frame, the two shutters and the window sill.

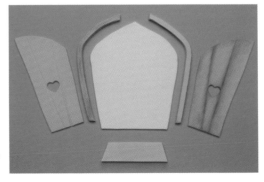

3. While the paste is still soft, cut out a small heart from the centre of each of the shutters using a cutter. Mark two lines down each shutter with the back of a knife or a ruler.

4. Dilute a little SK Brown QFC Paste with clear alcohol or cooled, boiled water and paint a wash over the shutters using downward strokes to resemble wood.

5. Allow the pieces to dry on a flat surface.

Wishing Fairy

For instructions on how to make a fairy, see pages 6 to 9.

1. Model the top half of the fairy's body from purple-coloured SFP. Insert a strand of spaghetti into the top.

2. Colour some SFP a flesh colour and model the head, neck and arms (I have not used a mould for this fairy).

3. Paint the face with diluted QFC Dusts using a no. 00 paintbrush. Give the fairy blue eyes, red lips and freckles. Allow all the pieces to dry.

4. Make the wings using the gelatine technique, following the template (see inside back cover). Colour the gelatine by adding a little Pink QFC Paste.

5. Assemble the fairy and window pieces and secure the fairy to the window with royal icing. Make a green fringe to hide the join around the neck.

6. Colour some royal icing yellow and place in a piping bag with a no. 5 nozzle. Pipe the hair onto the fairy and use a dampened no. 4 paintbrush to smooth the hair and give it movement.

7. Cut out several tiny blossoms from White SFP and colour the centres with a dot of diluted Red QFC Dust. Stick the flowers in place on the hair while the royal icing is still wet.

Flowers and Leaves

1. Make 11 small, wired flowers from pink SFP, following the instructions for fantasy flower no. 1 (see pages 9 to 11). Give each flower a blue stamen. Tape the wire using green floristry tape.

2. To make the wired blue flowers, follow the instructions for fantasy flower no. 3 (see pages 9 to 11). Make four altogether. Add a blue stamen to each and tape the wire, as before.

3. Make three wired white flowers, following the instructions for fantasy flower no. 4 (see pages 9 to 11). Make five blue stamens for each flower and tape the wire.

4. Make two pale pink flowers following the instructions for fantasy flower no. 2 (see pages 9 to 11). Add yellow stamens and tape the wire.

5. Roll out some pale green flower paste and cut out eight medium no. 1 fantasy leaves and 17 small no. 1 fantasy leaves (see pages 9 to 11). Wire each leaf and vein with a Great Impressions Honeysuckle Veiner. Allow to dry.

Butterflies

1. To make the two butterflies, thinly roll out some White SFP. Cut out four wing shapes using the template (see inside back cover). Allow to dry flat.

2. When the wings of the butterfly are dry, use a fine paintbrush and QFC Dusts diluted with glaze cleaner or clear alcohol to paint the wings the desired colours. (Alternatively, you can use an airbrush to colour the wings.) Allow the colour to dry.

3. Colour a small amount of royal icing with Brown QFC Paste and pipe a body onto each butterfly to join the wings together. Whilst the icing is still wet, add two white stamens for the anthers. (You can colour the tips in the same way as for the flower stamens.)

Assembly

1. Secure the window and fairy to the top of the cake with royal icing.

2. Arrange the small flowers and leaves around the top of the window and secure in place with royal icing. Make a small spray for the base of the cake and place the other flowers in front of the fairy.

3. Secure the butterflies in place and support until dry if necessary.

The Fairytale

Materials

25.5cm x 35.5cm (10" x 14") rectangular cake
250g (9oz) SK Sugar Florist Paste (SFP): White
1kg (2lb 3oz) sugarpaste: white
SK QFC Dusts: Blue, Black, Brown, Green, Pink,
White and Yellow
SK QFC Pastes: Black, Blue, Brown, Green, Orange,
Pink, Purple, Red and White
Royal icing
SK Fairy Dust: Ice White
Gelatine solution (see pages 8 to 9)

Equipment

Non-stick board and rolling pin
SK Great Impressions Face Mould: Small
Sharp knife
CelStick
Fine scissors
SK Paintbrushes: nos. 00 and 4
Fantasy flower cutters: nos. 2, 4 and 5 (see pages
9 to 11)
SK Great Impressions Sweet Pea Veiner
Fantasy Leaf cutter: no. 1 medium and small (see
pages 9 to 11)
SK Great Impressions Honeysuckle Veiner
24-gauge floristry wires: green
Floristry tape: green
Wire cutters
Piping nozzle: no. 3
Piping bag
SK Glaze Cleaner (IPA) or clear alcohol
Nylon thread
PVA glue
Wooden skewer (food-grade)
30.5cm x 40.5cm (12" x 16") rectangular cake
drum, carved to shape
145cm (57") x 1.5cm width ribbon: purple

Method

Covering the Cake and Board

1. Carve the top of the cake to resemble an open book. Cover the cake with white sugarpaste and mark the sides of the cake with a CelStick to resemble the pages. Allow to firm.

2. Colour the remaining sugarpaste with Purple QFC Paste and cover the shaped cake drum. Allow to firm.

3. Position the cake centrally on the drum. Trim the edge of the cake drum with purple ribbon.

Fairytale Scene

1. Using QFC Dusts diluted with glaze cleaner or clear alcohol, paint a landscape onto the right-hand side of the cake. You can use the picture shown here as a guide, or create your own scene. Allow to dry.

 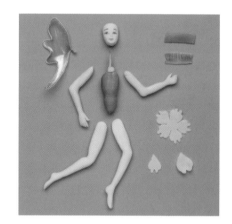

2. To add texture to the picture, paint on the tree and cloud in royal icing using a no. 4 paintbrush. You will need to colour the icing for the tree with Brown QFC Paste.

3. Use Blue QFC Paste and a no. 4 paintbrush to start the fairytale, "Once upon a time…" on the left hand side. Make sure the final letter finishes just below the centre of the page so that the quill pen can be inserted later.

Bookmark

1. Colour some SFP a pale lilac colour using Purple QFC Paste. Roll out a long strip and cut the edges straight.

2. Using Purple QFC Paste and a no. 00 paintbrush, add some decoration to the bookmark. Lay it down the centre of the book and allow to dry.

Storybook Fairies

For instructions on how to make a fairy, see pages 6 to 9.

1. Make three small bodies in green SFP.

2. Model the heads, arms and legs in flesh-coloured SFP. Bend the arms and legs of the fairies into different positions.

3. Paint the faces on the fairies with diluted QFC Dusts using a no. 00 paintbrush.

4. Allow all the pieces to dry, then assemble the fairies using royal icing.

5. To make the skirts, thinly roll out some pink SFP. Cut out three blossoms using a no. 4 fantasy flower cutter (see pages 9 to 11) and separate each petal using a sharp knife. Thin the petals further, then secure 15 petals around the waist of each fairy.

6. Make three pairs of wings using the gelatine technique, following the template (see inside back cover). Add Pink QFC to the gelatine solution to colour the wings. Allow to dry.

7. Roll out a long strip of green SFP and cut a fringe with a pair of fine scissors. Secure around the neck and waist of each fairy.

8. Make up some royal icing in three colours: yellow, brown and dark brown. Place the icing in three piping bags, each with a no. 3 piping nozzle, and pipe the hair onto the fairies. Use a no. 4 paintbrush dampened with cooled, boiled water to smooth the hair and give it movement.

Quill Pen

1. Roll out some White SFP and cut out the feather shape, following the step photograph as a guide. Texture down both sides of the feather with a CelStick, keeping the feather at an angle.

2. Brush a little cooled, boiled water down the centre of the back of the feather. Place a wooden skewer into the centre and bring the paste around it to secure it in place. The pointed end should protrude approximately 5cm (2") at the base of the feather (this will be inserted into the cake later). Allow the feather to dry.

3. Using Blue and Black QFC Dusts diluted with glaze cleaner or clear alcohol, paint the feather with a no. 00 paintbrush. Paint the skewer at the base with Blue QFC Paste to resemble the ink on the quill pen.

Flowers

1. Make six pink flowers following the instructions for fantasy flower no. 2 (see pages 9 to 11). Insert five yellow stamens into each flower and tape a 24-gauge floristry wire onto each flower with green floristry tape.

2. Make six white flowers following the instructions for fantasy flower no. 5 (see pages 9 to 11). Dust the centre of each flower pale green and make seven orange stamens for each one.

3. Make approximately 10 small and 22 medium no. 1 fantasy leaves in green SFP. Wire and vein each leaf, then dust various shades of green.

Assembly

1. Insert the pointed end of the quill pen into the cake at an angle. Position one of the fairies so that she is holding the feather.

2. Wire the flowers into three small sprays and place them into position, taking care not to insert any of the wires into the cake.

3. Place the two remaining fairies into position beside the flower sprays.

IMPORTANT NOTE: Remember to remove the wooden skewer before the cake is served.

A New Arrival

Materials

25.5cm x 35.5cm (10" x 14") rectangular cake
250g (9oz) SK Sugar Florist Paste (SFP): White
250g (9oz) SK Marzipan
1kg (2lb 3oz) sugarpaste: white
100g (3½oz) Squires Kitchen Mexican Modelling
Paste (MMP): White
SK QFC Dusts: Black, Blue, Brown, Green, Orange,
Red and White
SK QFC Pastes: Green, Orange, Pink, Red, White and
Yellow
SK Professional Liquid or Dust Colour: Fern
Royal icing
Gelatine solution (see pages 8 to 9)
SK Fairy Dust: Ice White
SK Edible Glue

Equipment

Non-stick board and rolling pin
Airbrush (optional)
SK Great Impressions Face Moulds: Medium and
Extra Small
SK Paintbrushes: nos. 00 and 4
CelStick
Fantasy flower cutters: nos. 1 and 5 (see pages
9 to 11)
Fantasy leaf cutter: no. 1 medium (see pages 9 to 11)
SK Great Impressions Honeysuckle Veiner
Tiny blossom cutter (OP, no. F2S)
Piping nozzle: no. 3
Piping bag
SK Confectioners' Glaze (IPA)
PVA glue
Floristry tape: green
Floristry wire
30.5cm x 40.5cm (12" x 16") rectangular cake drum,
carved to shape
145cm (57") x 1.5cm width ribbon: dark green
CelStick

Method

Covering the Cake and Board

1. Cover the cake with white sugarpaste. Colour the remaining sugarpaste with Green QFC Paste and cover the board. Allow to firm.

2. Position the cake centrally on the board. Trim the edge of the board with dark green ribbon.

3. Colour the top of the cake green using Fern Dust Food Colour and a flat brush or use an airbrush with Fern Liquid Food Colour.

4. Using Green QFC Paste and a no. 00 paintbrush, paint grass on the sides of the cake and allow to dry.

Woodland Fairy

For instructions on how to make a fairy, see pages 6 to 9.

1. Make a medium body from green-coloured SFP.

2. Colour the paste for the fairy's head and limbs and add an extra 10g of paste to make the baby later. Make the face, arms and legs of the fairy, bending the legs into a kneeling position and arranging the arms as if the fairy is about to pick up the baby.

3. Paint the fairy's face with diluted QFC Dusts using a no. 00 paintbrush.

4. Allow all the pieces to dry and then assemble the fairy, using royal icing to secure the pieces together.

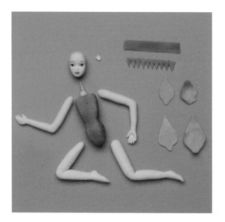

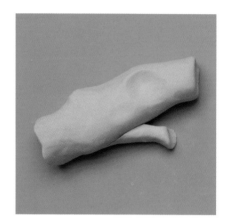

5. Roll out some orange-coloured SFP thinly and cut out 16 petals using fantasy flower cutter no. 5. Arrange the petals around the waist, making the skirt.

6. Roll out a long strip of green SFP and cut a fringe with a pair of fine scissors. Secure around the neck and waist of the fairy.

7. Make the wings using the gelatine technique, following the template (see inside back cover). Add a little Pink QFC Paste to the solution to make the wings pink.

8. Colour some royal icing with Brown QFC Paste and place in a piping bag with a no. 3 nozzle. Pipe the hair onto the fairy's head and use a no. 4 paintbrush dampened with cooled, boiled water to smooth the hair and give it movement.

9. Make four tiny blossoms from pale pink SFP. Secure two to the fairy's head whilst the hair is still wet and keep the others for the baby.

Tree Trunk

1. Model a cylinder from MMP measuring approximately 6cm (2½") in diameter and 15cm (6") in length. Allow to firm.

2. Colour some SFP with Brown QFC Paste and roll out to a thickness of 0.5cm ($^1/_8$"). Cut out a rectangle that will cover the surface of the cylinder. Allow the paste to dry for several minutes, then stretch the paste with your fingers, causing the surface to crack and resemble bark.

3. Brush the MMP cylinder with cooled, boiled water and wrap the cracked SFP around it. Trim the join.

4. Paint a bark effect onto the paste using SK Brown and Black QFC Pastes.

Bees

1. To make a bee, roll a cone shape of yellow SFP for the body and a ball for the head. Stick two small strips of brown SFP onto the body, then paint the eyes with Black QFC Paste. You will need to make five bees altogether.

2. To make the anthers, cut two short pieces of wire and attach a tiny ball of black SFP to one end. Push the anthers into the head.

3. To make the wings, create a film of gelatine in any shape using the same technique as for the fairy wings (see pages 8 to 9). Allow the gelatine to dry, then cut the tiny wing shapes out with a pair of fine scissors. Stick them in place with a tiny amount of SK Edible Glue.

Ladybirds

1. To make a ladybird, roll a ball of red SFP measuring approximately 1.5cm (⁵⁄₈") in diameter. Using a CelStick, mark down the centre of the paste. Make eight altogether.

2. Roll several tiny balls of black SFP and stick them onto the ladybirds. Make the heads from the same paste and paint on the eyes and mouth with diluted White QFC Dust.

3. Make the wings from gelatine in the same way as for the bees and secure in place.

Flowers and Leaves

1. To make the tiny yellow flowers, roll out some yellow SFP and follow the instructions for fantasy flower no. 1 (see pages 9 to 11). Give each flower one red stamen and tape to a 26-gauge wire using green floristry tape. You will need to make ten flowers altogether.

2. To make the larger yellow and orange flowers, follow the instructions for fantasy flower no. 5 (see pages 9 to 11). You will need to make four of each colour. Give both the yellow and orange flowers between five and seven red stamens each, then paint red or orange dots on the petals using diluted QFC Dusts. Tape a 24-gauge wire to each flower.

3. Make approximately eight medium no. 1 fantasy leaves from green SFP (see pages 9 to 11). Vein and wire each one.

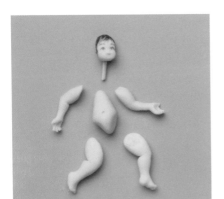

Baby Fairy

1. Use the extra flesh-coloured SFP made earlier to make the baby. For the body, model a cone measuring approximately 1.5cm (⅝") across and 2cm (¾") long.

2. Make the head and limbs, using the step photograph as a guide. Make the wings from gelatine, using the template as a guide (see inside back cover).

3. Paint the face with diluted QFC Dusts using a no. 00 paintbrush. Stick two tiny blossoms to the fairy's head.

4. Allow all the pieces to dry and then secure them together with royal icing.

Assembly

1. Roll several small balls of brown and grey sugarpaste, MMP or SFP (you can use any leftover pieces of paste for this). Stick the stones and some of the small flowers around the base of the cake with dots of royal icing. Add some of the larger flowers and leaves at the front of the cake.

2. Place the tree trunk in the centre of the cake and arrange a few flowers around it. To make the nest, colour some SFP pale yellow and roll several tapered sausage shapes. Arrange the nest on top of the trunk.

3. Place the baby fairy in the nest. Position the mother fairy as if she is about to pick up the baby. Secure the fairy's legs to the tree trunk with royal icing.

4. Stick the bees and the ladybirds to the cake and the board.

The Mermaid Ball

Materials

30.5cm x 25.5cm (12" x 10") oval cake

250g (9oz) SK Sugar Florist Paste (SFP): White

500g (1lb 1oz) SK Pastillage

1kg (2lb 3oz) sugarpaste: white

SK QFC Dusts: Black, Blue, Brown, Orange, Pink and White

SK QFC Pastes: Black, Blue, Brown, Green, Orange, Pink, Purple, Red, White and Yellow

SK Professional Liquid or Dust Food Colour: Gentian

SK Fairy Dust: Ice White

SK Piping Gel

Gelatine solution (see pages 8 to 9)

Royal icing

Equipment

Non-stick board and rolling pin

Airbrush (optional)

SK Great Impressions Face Mould: Medium

Modelling tools (PME)

SK Paintbrushes: nos. 00 and 4

Piping nozzles: no. 3

Piping bag

SK Glaze Cleaner (IPA)

PVA glue

Wooden skewers (food-grade)

CelStick

Curved former

55cm (21") x 1.5cm width ribbon: pale blue

35.5cm x 30.5cm (14" x 12") oval cake drum

Method

Covering the Cake and Board

1. Cover the cake with white sugarpaste. Add a hint of Purple and Blue QFC Pastes to the sugarpaste and use this to cover the board. Allow both the cake and board to dry and then place the cake centrally on the board.

2. Airbrush or dust the cake in shades of blue to represent the sea.

3. Cover the edge of the board with blue ribbon.

Rocks

1. Make several rocks from pastillage, following the method for rock sugar (see pages 4 to 5).

2. Insert three wooden skewers into the cake and thread the pastillage rocks onto them to create tall pillars.

Mermaids

For instructions on how to make a fairy, see pages 6 to 9.

1. Make medium-sized heads, arms and bodies for the three mermaids from flesh-coloured SFP.

2. Model the mermaids' tails from SFP coloured in different pastel shades, using the step picture as a guide. Save a little of each colour to make the shells and belt. Arrange the tails in different positions.

3. Paint the faces of the mermaids with diluted QFC Dusts using a no. 00 paintbrush.

4. Allow all the pieces to dry. When dry, assemble the mermaids using royal icing.

5. Model two conch shells and a belt for each mermaid using the paste reserved earlier. Secure the shells to the mermaids' chests and wrap the belts around their waists to hide the join between the body and tail.

6. Prepare some royal icing, divide into three and colour yellow, brown and dark brown. Place each colour in a piping bag with a no. 3 nozzle and pipe the hair onto the mermaids. Use a no. 4 paintbrush dampened with cooled, boiled water to smooth the hair and give it movement.

Coral and Seaweed

1. Model the coral shapes in pastillage and texture the surface of the paste with a ball tool. While the paste is still soft, insert a cocktail stick into some of the corals so that they can stand upright on top of the cake.

2. Colour some SFP yellow and model the conch shells, starfish and seashells. Use a CelStick to create the texture. Allow to dry, then dust with a hint of Orange QFC Dust.

3. Roll out some green SFP and cut long, thin strands for the seaweed. Allow to dry on a curved former to give movement.

Assembly

1. Secure several rocks, shells and starfish around the base of the cake to cover the join.

2. Place the three mermaids on top of the cake and add the remaining rocks, coral, starfish, shells and seaweed around them. Secure all the pieces in place with royal icing.

3. Place some clear piping gel in a piping bag, snip off the tip and pipe drops onto the cake and board to resemble water. Allow to dry.

IMPORTANT NOTE: Remember to remove the wooden skewers and cocktail sticks before the cake is served.

Suppliers

Shops (UK/Europe)

CelCakes & CelCrafts (CC)
Springfield House
Gate Helmsley
York YO41 1NF
UK
Tel: +44 (0)1759 371 447
Email: info@celcrafts.co.uk
Website: www.celcrafts.co.uk

Confectionery Supplies (Tinkertech Two) (TT)
Unit 11a, b and c
Foley Trading Estate
Hereford HR1 2SF
UK
Tel: +44 (0)1432 371 451/+44 (0)29 2037 2161 (mail order)
Email: kclements@btinternet.com
Website: www.confectionerysupplies.co.uk

FMM Sugarcraft (FMM)
Unit 5
Kings Park Industrial Estate
Primrose Hill
Kings Langley
Hertfordshire WD4 ST8
UK
Tel: +44 (0)1923 268 699
Email: clements@f-m-m.demon.co.uk
Website: www.fmmsugarcraft.com

Orchard Products (OP)
51 Hallyburton Road
Hove
East Sussex BN3 7GP
UK
Tel: 0800 9158 226 /
+44 (0)1273 419 418
Email: enquiries@orchardproducts.co.uk
Website: www.orchardproducts.co.uk

Squires Kitchen Sugarcraft (SK)
Squires House
3 Waverley Lane
Farnham
Surrey GU9 8BB
UK
Tel: 0845 22 55 67 1/2 (from UK)/
+44 (0)1252 711 749 (from overseas)
Email: info@squires-group.co.uk
Online shop: www.squires-shop.com
Website: www.squires-group.co.uk

Tårtdecor
Bulygatan 14
442 40 KUNGÄLV
Sweden
Tel: +46 303 514 70
Email: info@tartdecor.se
Website: www.tartdecor.se

Shops (Argentina)

CAIRO
Corvalán 3343 (1439) Capital Federal
Argentina
Tel/fax: 00-54-11-602-7368
Email: cairo@infovia.com.ar
Website: www.cortantescairo.com

Cecilia Morana's School
Virrey Avilés 3007 - (1426) Capital Federal
Argentina
Tel/fax: 00-54-11-4554-7312
Email: cecilia_morana@ciudad.com.ar
Website: www.cecilia-morana.com.ar

FLEIBOR
30 de agosto 162 (1766) La Tablada
Buenos Aires
Argentina
Tel/fax: 00-54-11-4652-8035
Email: fleibor@speedy.com.ar
Website: www.laboraratoriofleibor.com.ar

Laboratorio DEWEY
General Hornos 333 (1752) Lomas del Mirador
Buenos Aires
Argentina
Tel/fax: 00-54-11-4454-7200/7127
Email: contacto@deweyargentina.com.ar
Website: www.deweyargentina.com.ar

Distributors

Culpitt Ltd.
Tel: +44 (0)1670 814 545
Email: info@culpitt.com
Website: www.culpitt.com

Guy, Paul & Co. Ltd.
Tel: +44 (0)1494 432 121
Email: sales@guypaul.co.uk
Website: www.guypaul.co.uk

Squires Kitchen Sugarcraft (SK)
(See left)

Manufacturers

AP Cutters (AP)
Tel: +44 (0)1934 812 787

PME Ltd.
Tel: +44 (0)20 8864 0888
Email: enquiry@pmeltd.co.uk
www.pmeltd.co.uk

Squires Kitchen Sugarcraft (SK)
(See left)